John Muir

By Wil Mara

Consultants

Nanci R. Vargus, Ed.D.
Primary Multiage Teacher
Decatur Township Schools, Indianapolis, Indiana

Katharine A. Kane, Reading Specialist
Former Language Arts Coordinator
San Diego County Office of Education

P Children's Press ®
A Division of Scholastic Inc.
New York   Toronto   London   Auckland   Sydney
Mexico City   New Delhi   Hong Kong
Danbury, Connecticut

Designer: Herman Adler Design
Photo Researcher: Caroline Anderson
The photo on the cover shows John Muir.

Library of Congress Cataloging-in-Publication Data

Mara, Wil.
 John Muir / by Wil Mara.
   p. cm. — (Rookie biographies)
Summary: Introduces the life of John Muir, the naturalist who formed the
Sierra Club to help preserve the Sierra Mountains.
  ISBN 0-516-22515-4 (lib. bdg.)   0-516-27342-6 (pbk.)
  1. Muir, John, 1838-1914—Juvenile literature. 2. Naturalists—United
States—Biography—Juvenile literature. 3. Conservationists—United
States—Biography—Juvenile literature. [1. Muir, John, 1838-1914.
2. Naturalists. 3. Conservationists.] I. Title. II. Series.
  QH31.M9 M255 2002
  333.7'2'092—dc21

                                    2001008317

1 2 3 4 5 6 7 8 9 10 R 11 10 09 08 07 06 05 04 03 02

Can you imagine living
in the woods?

John Muir spent many years doing this. He was a naturalist (NACH-ur-uh-list). A naturalist is someone who cares about nature.

Muir was born in the country of Scotland in 1838. As a boy he spent many hours with his brother, David, playing in the Scottish hills.

In 1849, Muir's father moved the family to America. He thought they would be happier there. The Muirs bought a farm in Wisconsin.

Muir had to do a lot of hard work on the farm. He did not like this. When he was 22 years old he left the farm so he could go to the University of Wisconsin.

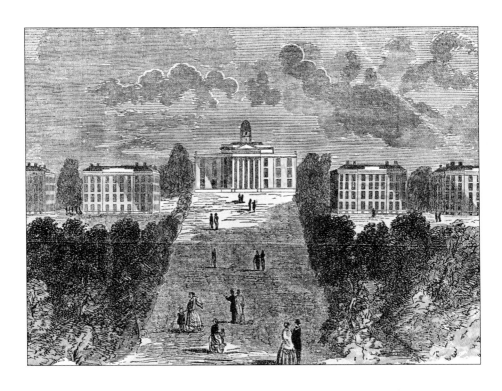

11

12

At school, Muir learned about many different types of plants and animals. Soon he wanted to see them for real.

He left the University of Wisconsin in 1863 and began hiking through forests and valleys. He collected flowers and plants. He also wrote about his trip in notebooks.

Dry Creek on whose happy bank my Cabin stands is subject to sudden swellings & overflows in the rainy season. Then it becomes a majestic stream almost a river with serious & confident gestures, curving about its jutting banks & horseshoe bends carrying fences & hedge timbers & all carries logs & houses within reach of its channel power. In the course of a few hours after the close of a rain it will retire within its to its narrow beaten leaving many flat smooth beach sheets of sand. I like to watch the first writings upon these fresh new made leaflets of Nature own. One of these pages was made last night & was already written upon when I saw it this morning. It is

In 1868 he arrived in California. Muir went to the Sierra Nevada Mountains. He thought it was the most beautiful place in the world.

Muir lived in the Sierra Mountains for years. He built a cabin. He studied the animals and plants. He drank water from rivers. He ate whatever fruits and vegetables he could grow.

Some people did not care about the Sierra Mountains. They wanted to cut down the trees and build dams. A dam is a wall that stops a river from flowing.

Muir found other people who cared about the Sierras. He got them together in a group and called it the Sierra Club.

23

The Sierra Club members wanted to create laws that would protect the Sierras. In 1903 John Muir visited these mountains with President Theodore Roosevelt (THEE-uh-dor ROZE-uh-velt). The president loved what he saw and promised to help Muir keep the mountains safe.

John Muir died in California on December 24, 1914.

"CLIMB THE MOUNTAINS AND GET THEIR GOOD TIDINGS
NATURE'S PEACE   WILL FLOW INTO YOU
AS SUNSHINE   FLOWS INTO TREES
THE WINDS WILL   BLOW THEIR OWN
FRESHNESS INTO YOU   AND THE STORMS
THEIR ENERGY   WHILE CARES WILL
DROP OFF LIKE   AUTUMN LEAVES"

JOHN MUIR

BUILT HERE A SUGAR PINE CABIN IN 1869
AND MADE IT HIS HOME FOR TWO YEARS

IN COMMEMORATION OF THE NOBLE
SERVICE WHICH THIS FRIEND AND PRO-
TECTOR OF NATURE RENDERED TO THE
PEOPLE OF THE UNITED STATES THIS
TABLET HAS BEEN PLACED HERE IN
1924 BY THE CALIFORNIA CONFERENCE
OF SOCIAL WORK R. Nolti Burnham

Today the Sierra Club is bigger than ever. It protects wild places all over the world. John Muir made it for anyone who cares about nature. Even you can join!

Words You Know

dam

journal

John Muir

naturalist

30

President Theodore Roosevelt

Scotland

Sierra Club

Sierra Mountains

31

Index

About the Author

Wil Mara has written over fifty books. His works include both fiction and nonfiction for children and adults. He lives with his wife and three daughters in northern New Jersey.

Photo Credits

DATE DUE

921
MUI

Mara, Wil.

John Muir

$12.95

Moravia Park Pre K–8 Campus
12 /03 /2003